Savvy

Fashion
FORWARD

COOL CAT

Bringing 1940s and 1950s Flair to Your Wardrobe

by Lori Luster

Consultant:
Hazel Clark, PhD
Research Chair of Fashion
Parsons The New School for Design
New York, New York

CAPSTONE PRESS
a capstone imprint

Savvy Books are published by Capstone Press,
1710 Roe Crest Drive, North Mankato, Minnesota 56003
www.capstonepub.com

Library of Congress Cataloging-in-Publication Data
Luster, Lori.
Cool cat : bringing 1940s and 1950s flair to your wardrobe / by Lori Luster.
pages cm—(Savvy. Fashion forward)
Includes bibliographical references and index.
Summary: "Describes the fashion trends of the 1940s and 1950s, including step-by-step instructions on how to get the looks today"—Provided by publisher.
ISBN 978-1-4765-3998-0 (library binding) — ISBN 978-1-4765-6159-2 (ebook pdf)
1. Dress accessories—Juvenile literature. 2. Fashion—United States—History—20th century. I. Title.
TT649.8.L87 2014
746.9'2—dc23

2013028498

Editorial Credits
Jennifer Besel, editor; Tracy Davies McCabe, designer; Marcie Spence, media researcher;
    Jennifer Walker, production specialist

Photo Credits
Alamy Images: AF Archive, 52, Everett Collection Historical, 34 (left); Art Resource, N.Y.: The Metropolitan Museum of Art, New York, NY, USA, 16, 36 (left); Capstone Studio: Karon Dubke, 5, 13, 17 (stockings), 21, 24, 25, 27, 31, 37, 39, 43; Corbis: Bettmann, 44, David Lees, 23, Splash News, 47 (top); Getty Images: Adam Glickman/Underwood Archives, 10, Alfred Eisenstaedt/Time & Life Pictures, 14, 22-23, Allan Grant/Time Life Pictures, 54, Bert Hardy/Picture Post/Hulton Archive, 18 (left), Chaloner Woods, 48 (left), Cindy Ord, 48 (right), Dean Conger/The Denver Post, 30 (left), Dinodia, 12 (left), George Hurrell/John Kobal Foundation, 51, George Marks/Retrofile, 29, George Skadding/Time Life Pictures, 8 (left), Harold M. Lambert, 26, John Kobal Foundation, 6, 58 (left), Kathleen Revis/National Geographic, 38, Keystone-France/Gamma-Keystone, 32, Mark Rucker/Transcendental Graphics, 46, Michel Dufour/WireImage, 34 (right), Nina Leen/Time Life Pictures, 4, 56, Steve Granitz/WireImage, 45 (left), Warner Brothers, 40 (left); iStockphoto: kevinruss, 49 (top); Shutterstock: Adisa, 17 (shoes), Africa Studio, 57, andersphoto, 15 (left), Apostrophe, design element, Bwilson, 49 (bottom), Cherkas, 17 (coat), cretolamna, 9 (bag), DFree, 59, Dostoevsky, 35 (pearls), elic, design element, Elnur, 35 (shoes), 41 (shoes), Everett Collection, 47 (bottom), Featureflash, 36 (right), 45 (right), 58 (right), 60 (right), 61 (left), Flamestar, 19 (comb), fuyu liu, cover (scarf), glamour, 41 (shirt), Gnilenkov Aleksey, 19 (hat), Helga Esteb, 7 (tight), 12 (right), 53 (middle), 60 (left), Helga Pataki, design element, ilzesgimene, 9 (shoes), Jaguar PS, 40 (right), Joe Seer, 60 (middle), Juergen Faelchle, design element, Karkas, 9 (skirt), 17 (dress), 35 (dress), 41 (jeans), kavring, 35 (bag), Kaya, 41 (scarf), Leila B., 9 (shirt), Lucy Liu, 41 (flower), Nataliia Litovchenko, design element, photobank.kiev.ua, cover (left), Roberto Castillo, design element, s_bukley, 7 (left), 8 (right), 11, 15 (right), 18 (right), 19 (top), 30 (right), 33, 53 (left and right), 55, 61 (right), Swill Klitch, design element, tanuha2001, 19 (clip), tukkki, design element, Zaneta Baranowska, 35 (gloves)

Printed in the United States of America in Brainerd, Minnesota.
092013   007770BANGS14

Table of
Contents

MODERN RETRO

Believe it or not, the trends you're wearing right now aren't entirely new. Look at the cuffed jeans and capris folded in your drawer. Put on a pair of wedge shoes. Tie your hair up in a scarf and paint your nails. All these trends are retro looks that started in the 1940s and 1950s.

The '40s and '50s were a time of enormous change for fashion in the United States. A young generation of Americans was dancing to swing music and rock and roll. Everyone was healing from the failed banks, food shortages, and no jobs of the 1930s' Great Depression. Men went to fight in World War II (1939–1945).

Suddenly women had new roles at home and in the workplace. All these changes had a deep and lasting effect on fashion.

The '40s and '50s ushered in new fashions that continue to influence styles. If you have blue jeans or a bikini, you're wearing trends that began in these decades. The looks that originated in the '40s and '50s are ageless, and that's why they are still popular today.

You can bring even more of the iconic styles of these decades into your look. From styling your hair to making your own poodle skirt, what was old is new again!

COMFORTABLE ELEGANCE

In the early 1940s, people across the United States were struggling to rebuild their lives after the Great Depression. Americans turned to music and films as a way to cope with the difficult times, and both influenced the styles of the day.

In 1940 American clothing styles were dominated by the Paris couture houses. Designers Jeanne Lanvin, Coco Chanel, and Madeleine Vionnet created the styles of the day. At the beginning of the decade, the popularity of Lanvin's romantic tiny waists and swirling full skirts grew.

Chanel's beautiful use of simple lines hugging the body and comfortable fabrics was still as sought out and admired as it was in the 1930s.

But American couture clothing by this time was also greatly inspired by Madeleine Vionnet. Vionnet's revolutionary bias cut is still used on apparel worn today. Look at any material, and you'll notice that it is made of woven fibers. Material that is cut on the bias is cut at an angle across its weave. This cut causes the material to drape and hang. Draping creates a more flowing and graceful look to fabrics. It also tailors to your body in a flattering way.

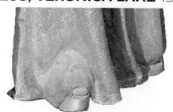

ACTRESS, VERONICA LAKE 1942

Bias cut dresses are as popular today was they were in the 1940s. Stars such as Miley Cyrus and Amber Riley wear this style to show off their shapes.

Dancing in a New Style

As dancing changed, so did clothing.

New trends in music and dance brought about changes in fashion styles. America's youth was jitterbugging to swing music. For many, swing was much more than music—it was a lifestyle. Teens and young adults danced to cool hipster entertainers wearing zoot suits and playing innovative jazz with a pulsing beat.

Swing dancing had women flying in the air and swinging around dance floors. This style of dance was more athletic than styles that came before.

As dancing changed, so did clothing. Hems got a little shorter, hovering at the knee. Young women also started wearing fuller skirts with button-down blouses, which allowed for easier movement.

The cute, comfortable skirt and shirt ensembles of swing dancers has definitely not gone out of style. The combo is everywhere from the racks of local department stores to Hollywood's A-list actresses. Eva Mendes, Katie Holmes, and Jennifer Lawrence have all rocked the look.

PUT IT TOGETHER

The 1940s swing look is easy to throw together and is perfect for a summer outing.

Grab a white button-down blouse from your (or your Mom's) closet.

Check the thrift store for a fun, flowy knee-length skirt.

Do a search online for "low-heeled Mary Janes" to find a great pair of toe tappers.

Check an accessory story for a rectangular clutch to finish the look.

SLIPS and HOSE

Women in the 1940s changed what they wore under their clothes too. 1940s women began wearing supportive bras and rubberized girdles. Bras and girdles gave them freedom of movement while still slimming and shaping their bodies.

Women also wore slips with fuller skirts over the bra and girdle. Slips helped to protect the modesty of dancers as they flipped in the air.

Stockings were an essential part of women's wardrobes too. Nylon stockings hit the shelves in 1940. They were inexpensive, plus they fit well and looked good. Shops had a terrible time keeping them on shelves. Stockings had a seam along the back. A true lady always made sure her stocking seams were straight along the backs of her legs.

Nylons have fallen out of favor in recent years, but they haven't gone away completely. Catherine, Duchess of Cambridge, is '40s chic. Her famous "buttered leg" stockings honor the past with their sheer, silky, natural sheen. Megan Fox, Mischa Barton, and Hayden Panettiere have been spotted wearing nude-tone hosiery as well.

MEGAN FOX

11

Swinging Up-Dos

Dancers couldn't have their hair flying all over. Two hairstyles became the go-to looks in the 1940s. Women either pulled their hair back into a very fashionable chignon or pinned their hair into spit curls.

Chignons are coils of hair arranged around the back of the head. This look was very popular off the dance floor for day or evening styles too. Spit curls were made by wrapping pieces of hair around the finger and using spit to flatten the curl against the head.

Both hairstyles are still popular. Chignons are everywhere on the red carpet. Carrie Underwood, Emma Stone, Jennifer Hudson, and Eva Longoria are just a few of the celebs who've thrown back to the '40s for their looks.

Spit curls are more fun and less elegant than chignons. American Idol contestant Syesha Mercado wore this playful look. Of course, hair spray, not spit, kept her curls in place.

Chignons are everywhere on the red carpet.

Get the Look

With a little practice, chignons can be a fun way to bring 1940s style into your look.

SUPPLIES

- straight comb
- hot rollers
- elastic band
- 2 side combs
- bobby pins
- hair spray

1. Part your hair loosely on the side.
2. Roll your hair in hot rollers. If you have short bangs, use a curling iron to curl them in the direction of your part.
3. Once the rollers are cool, take them out. Gently comb out the curls, so they aren't little ringlets.
4. Part your hair in front of each ear, so you have three sections of hair. Tie the back section in a low ponytail. Take the left-side section of hair, and twist it toward the back of your head. Secure the hair in place with a side comb or bobby pins. Repeat on the right-side section of hair.
5. Take out the ponytail and divide that hair into three parts. Tie the middle section back into a ponytail.
6. Divide the hair in the ponytail into two sections. Roll one section up and pin in place. Roll the other section down and pin in place.
7. Loosely twist one side section of hair and bring it back toward the rolled hair. Pin the twist in place. Repeat with the other section of loose hair.
8. Use hair spray to keep the hair in place.

From **Big Screen** to Dinner Tables

Just like today, 1940s audiences were in love with films and the celebrities who starred in them. The styles worn by screen sirens such as Joan Crawford, Lana Turner, and Rita Hayworth represented romance and elegance. Starlet fashion of the 1940s was driven by American designer Gilbert Adrian. Adrian worked mostly for MGM Studios. His pouf-sleeves, shoulder padding, and other "tricks" could make a less-than-perfect body look perfect. He created the square shouldered look that was prominent in 1940s dresses and skirt suits. Modern-day stars such as Beyoncé, Jessica Alba, and Kim Kardashian keep Adrian's shoulder pad trend alive.

Adrian had a powerful influence on fashion. Women saw his designs on movie starlets and loved them. Department stores began using Adrian's designs to create garments for ordinary women.

In addition to shoulder pads, Adrian also created both the slouch and trench coats and the pillbox hat. His trench coat is still a must-have style. Every star, including Kate Hudson and Anne Hathaway, turn to this timeless trend.

KATE HUDSON   BEYONCÉ

Off the Rack......................

Coco Chanel created the idea of mix and match separates in the 1930s. But only the very wealthy could afford her couture prices. It was American designer Claire McCardell who created the revolutionary approach of affordable separates. These pieces were sized right "off the rack," or "ready-to-wear" for the general public. This was a groundbreaking idea. Before McCardell's line, clothing was generally made for each individual. Women either sewed their family's apparel or paid a tailor to do it. "Ready-to-wear" clothing was just that. It was ready to wear without additional sewing. This "off the rack" trend is how most people buy their clothes today.

One of McCardell's most famous pieces was the popover dress. This dress was comfortable and trendy. Women loved it. And they still do. Modern versions of the popover are still as popular as ever. Tank dresses with cinched waists are a new take on McCardell's design. Jessica Simpson's clothing line includes several of these modern popovers.

Norman Norell set the trends for ready-to-wear evening apparel. His simple and sophisticated looks gained him attention and respect. Before the 1930s, black was saved for funeral attire. Coco Chanel created a niche for the "little black dress" in the '30s. But Norell made black a popular color for all clothes. His love of black was bold, yet elegant, and appeared in most of his apparel.

One of Norell's lasting designs is the sequined sheath dress. He debuted the look in the early 1940s, and it's a trend that lasts today. Gwyneth Paltrow and Taylor Swift are just a couple of celebs who sparkled on the red carpet wearing this vintage '40s look.

MCCARDELL'S POPOVER DRESS

PUT IT TOGETHER

Pull together a Norell-inspired 1940s evening outfit, and dazzle the night.

Check the prom dress sections of thrift shops for a knee-length sequin sheath dress.

Wear a knee-length wool coat over the dress for a vintage Norell look. Your grandmother might have one of these in her closet.

Grab some simple, low-heeled black pumps. You can find these just about anywhere heels are sold.

Look for nude-colored nylons with a back seam at your local department stores.

3

THE WAR CHANGES EVERYTHING

In 1941 the United States entered World War II. The war completely changed American lifestyles. As the men went to fight, women were left to take over. Suddenly, women were recruited to do everything from welding aircraft to driving taxi cabs.

The war brought a lot of restrictions to the fashion world. Supplies were rationed or banned altogether. Japan was the main exporter of silk at the time. But Japan was also a U.S. enemy during the war. The government banned all silk items. Leather was reserved for soldiers' leather boots. Zippers and metal buttons almost disappeared. All metals were used to make weapons. The government also rationed fabric. A woman's dress could only use about 3 yards (3 meters) of fabric. That's less fabric than two king-sized pillow cases.

The war forced fashion into a simpler look. For women, the 1940s look featured broad shoulders and a tailored waist tucked into either a pencil or A-line skirt. Hems fell just below the knee.

Pencil skirts with tailored waists are everywhere, even today. You might have one in your closet for special events. And celebs wear them all the time. Selena Gomez and Hayden Panettiere love their pencil skirts.

Top It Off

Hats and hair decorations were the only allowable splurge during the war. Small angled pillbox hats, headbands, snoods, and bows were all the rage. Hats and other decorations are still fun to play with. Accessory stores carry tons of options. Duchess Catherine and other British royalty have been seen in a variety of fun and creative pillbox styles. Kelly Osbourne has rocked the hair bow.

KELLY OSBOURNE

PUT IT TOGETHER

Add a touch of '40s flair to your look by putting on one of these toppers.

Find hair combs, feathers, barrettes, bows, and headbands at accessory stores.

Snoods are crocheted nets that hold the hair back in a stylish way. These are easy to find online.

Make your own pillbox hat or dig through your grandma's attic to see if you can find one.

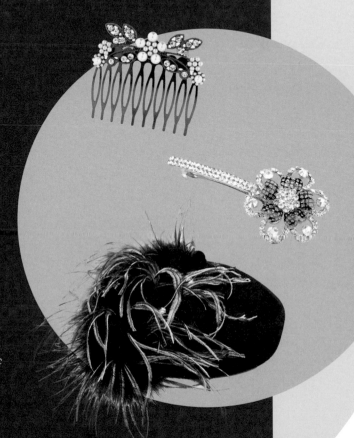

Get the Look

A pillbox hat is an essential accessory for the 1940s look. Make your own with a little bit of felt and a few stitches.

SUPPLIES

- math compass
- piece of copy paper
- scissors
- sewing pins
- 3 9x12-inch (23x30-centimeter) pieces of felt, all in the same color
- lightweight fusible interfacing
- piece of chalk or a marker
- sewing needle and a spool of thread matching your felt
- 12-inch (30-cm) long piece of ¾-inch (2-cm) wide elastic
- hot glue gun and glue
- silk flowers, netting, or feathers (optional)

1. Draw a circle on a piece of paper with the compass. The circle should be 7 inches (18 cm) across. Cut it out.
2. Pin the paper circle to one of the felt pieces. Using the paper circle as a pattern, cut out a felt circle. Repeat on another piece of felt and on the interfacing.
3. Mark a small "X" on one of the felt circles.
4. Lay the interface circle on top of the felt circle without the "X." Fuse the circles together according to the interfacing's package directions.
5. Lay the second felt circle on top of the interface circle. Keep the "X" side facing up. Sew all the way around the layered circles. Make your stitches as close to the edge as possible. Set the circle aside.

6. Draw two long rectangles on the remaining felt. Each rectangle should be 3 inches (8 cm) high and 20 inches (51 cm) long. Cut the rectangles out. Use one of the felt rectangles as a pattern to cut one out of the interfacing too.

7. Repeat steps 3–5 with the rectangles.

8. Lay the circle on your workspace, "X" side facing up. Pin the long edge of the rectangle around the edges of the circle. Make sure the "X" side of the rectangle faces out.

9. Sew the rectangle to the circle, going all the way around. When you get back to the start, carefully cut off any excess on the rectangle, leaving just ½ inch (1 cm) of fabric. Make a back seam on the hat by sewing the rectangle ends together.

10. Stitch the elastic around the base of the hat. Trim off any extra.

11. Flip the hat inside out.

12. Hot glue decorations to the hat, such as flowers, netting, or feathers.

Creative
Footwear

Shoe manufacturers had to get creative during wartime rationing. They developed new looks using natural materials such as cork, flax, straw, and wood instead of leather. Espadrilles made of canvas uppers and rope soles became very much in fashion. Today espadrilles are a summertime must-have for the Hollywood elite such as Jennifer Aniston.

Talented shoe makers such as Italian Salvatore Ferragamo used old furniture pieces for decoration. At the height of the war, Ferragamo's new creations used fishing line and packing string to make surprisingly innovative designs. Ferragamo's funky trends are still with us today. Check any shoe store, and look for shoes with stripes or unusual textures. Or look for wedges or platforms. Those shoes are all throwbacks to Ferragamo creations.

Get the Look

Make your own Ferragamo-inspired shoes for summer fun.

SUPPLIES

- craft knife
- pair of flip-flops
- heavy duty waterproof glue
- solid-color T-shirt
- ruler
- piece of chalk
- scissors
- screwdriver
- clothespins

1. With a craft knife, cut the flip-flop straps off. Leave the "plug" that goes between the toes in place. Be very careful using the craft knife. Always cut away from your body. And don't be afraid to get help from an adult.
2. Glue the toe plug in place.
3. Pop out the two strap plugs on the sides, leaving holes in the sole.
4. Lay the T-shirt out flat. Measure 2 inches (5 cm) up from the bottom hem, and make a chalk mark. Make about 4 more marks at the 2-inch (5-cm) height across the shirtfront. Cut along the marks, through both sides of the shirt. Then repeat the measuring and cutting so you have two 2-inch (5-cm) strips. The strips will be circular. Cut the circles so they are long strips.
5. Tie a knot at one end of one strip. Starting from the sole of the sandal, thread the strip through one plug hole. Use the screwdriver to push it through. The knot should nestle nicely into the hole. Glue the knot in place. Then tie a knot on the other end of the strip. Repeat with the second strip and plug hole.

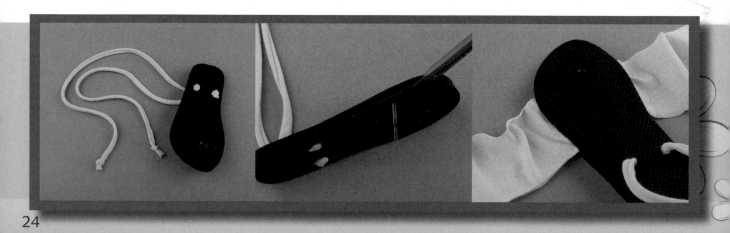

6. Turn the flip-flip sole up. Measure 1 inch (2.5 cm) down from the toe plug, and make a mark. Draw a horizontal line at the mark across the sandal.

7. Cut a horizontal slit that is 3 inches (8 cm) long and 1 inch (2.5 cm) deep on each side of the foam sole. The line you made in step 5 should be at the middle of the slits.

8. Measure 3 inches (8 cm) up from the bottom of the shirt and make a mark. Make about 4 more marks at the 3-inch (8-cm) height across the shirtfront. Cut the strip off through both sides of the shirt. Cut the circle so it's a long strip.

9. Lay the strip out on your workspace. Measure and cut the strip into two 8-inch (20-cm) long pieces.

10. Stuff one end of one 8-inch (20-cm) strip into a side slit. Use a ruler to push the fabric in. Repeat on the other side with the second strip.

11. Glue the strips into the slits. Clamp the strips in place with clothespins while they dry.

12. Wait at least 24 hours for the glue to completely dry before wearing the shoes. When putting on the sandals, tie the toe straps in a bow to fit your feet. Then tie the ankle straps.

Working Women

Throughout American history women had been barred from jobs that paid well or had status. Congress even passed laws that kept married women from getting jobs during the Great Depression of the 1930s. But World War II changed women's place in society. Thousands of American men left to fight in Europe. Women had to keep the factories and other businesses running. By the end of the war, at least 18 million women had joined the work force.

These hardworking ladies were called Rosies. A popular song of the time described "Rosie the Riveter," who worked for victory. Rosies became the symbol of women supporting the American war effort. These women left their popover dresses and heels at home. They tied up their hair and wore dungarees, or denim-pant coveralls, gloves, and protective goggles. The tied up hair and denim look came to represent the proud, hardworking women who still found ways to look pretty.

Get the Look

Hardworking women needed to keep their hair back, but also wanted to look good. The tied head scarf was a popular solution.

SUPPLIES

• a large head scarf

1. Fold the scarf in half diagonally.
2. Hold the scarf behind your head, with the point of the triangle pointing down.
3. Position the scarf under your hair. Pull the two ends up and tie them together on top of your head. Leave the ends loose.
4. Pull the triangle tip up to the top of your head. Stuff all your hair into the pouch.
5. Tie the two ends of the scarf over the triangle point to hold it in place. It may help if a partner holds the point down.
6. Tuck the sides of the scarf in.

MORE MONEY, MORE FASHION

On September 2, 1945, World War II officially ended. It took a while for life to return to normal after the war. After all, 6.2 million employed women left the work force and returned to their roles as wives and stay-at-home mothers. Men came back to the jobs they had left during the war. Even though the wartime rationing of goods had stopped, many goods remained in short supply for many months afterward.

That same year tensions between the United States and the Soviet Union brought the countries into what became known as the Cold War. The United States thought that the Soviets were spying on them. The American government and public grew paranoid. Strict new rules about how to act and what to look like dominated American society during the 1950s. Maintaining a polished appearance became very important. Advertisements showed women cleaning the house in heels and men eating supper in suits. These ads showed how the ideal family should look and behave.

By 1950 the American economy had grown very strong. This economic boom created a new era of prosperity for the United States. For the first time in many years, families had free time and money to spend.

A **Fur** Trend

During the 1950s fur coats became a status symbol for the average woman. Having a mink stole or fox cape gave the impression that a family was successful. Fur became such a symbol of wealth that women wore fur even if they lived in warm places.

Today, fur or faux fur stoles and wraps are still fashionable. A-listers, such as Jennifer Lopez, Paris Hilton, and Mary J. Blige, have all accented their looks with fur.

Fur coats became a status symbol for the average woman.

Get the Look

Get the wealthy 1950s fur stole look without breaking the bank.

SUPPLIES

- 1¾ yards (1.6 m) faux fur
- pins
- sewing needle and a spool of thread matching your fur color
- a thimble

1. Fold the faux fur lengthwise with the fur facing inside. Pin the long sides in place, leaving both ends open.
2. Sew along the long end so you end up with a long tube. Use the thimble to protect your thumb. The fur will be thick.
3. Refold the tube so the seam is in the center. Pin one short end together and sew it closed.
4. Put your hand inside the tube through the open end. Carefully pull the sewed end out to turn the stole right-side out.
5. Pin the open end closed and sew it shut. Use small stitches that camouflage well under the fur.

Dior's New Look

*a*fter the war women wanted to indulge their fashionable side. Fashion designer Christian Dior celebrated this new attitude with his "New Look." Dior created garments that defined excess. Some of his dresses featured calf-length crinoline skirts that used up to 80 yards (73 m) of fabric. That much fabric could almost cover a football field.

Dior's look took the fashion world by storm. After the boxy, plain looks of World War II, his creations were refreshing. However, the New Look required that women wear a girdle and cinch their waists with a corset. Dior's designs featured the hourglass figure—a large bosom, tiny waist, and full hips. For the correct effect, his full skirts required stiffened bodices and slip petticoats.

Waists in the 1950s were astonishingly small. Today's trendsetters don't wear waists quite so tight. But the 1950s full skirt and cinched waists are still popular. Zooey Deschanel and Emma Watson have both twirled this look on the red carpet.

ZOOEY
DESCHANEL

33

For day wear ladies also loved Dior's S-Line. Dior's S-Line was a sculpted hobble two-piece skirt suit. Hobble skirts are very similar to pencil skirts, but the hem is mid-calf and the slit in the back is very small or non-existent. Hobble skirts got their name from the restrictive way it makes a woman move.

Hobble skirts aren't the most comfortable fashion, but they are a lasting one. Solange Knowles and Anne Hathaway have pulled this look off. In 2011 the Chanel brand brought back the hobble skirt in some creative ways too.

Women accessorized the hourglass waist and S-Line looks with cute hats, gloves, and spiked stiletto heels. A pearl necklace with matching clip-on earrings and a coordinated handbag finished the look.

PUT IT TOGETHER

This fun, sophisticated outfit is perfect for a school dance or just a fancy evening with friends.

Look for a dress with a fitted bodice and flared skirt at your local department store.

Check your grandma's closet for a vintage 1950s handbag. Or find a rectangle-shaped bag at an accessory store.

Accessory stores carry gloves and pearl necklace and earring sets to polish off your outfit.

Browse your local shoe stores for spiked heels to compliment your dress.

Balenciaga's
Timeless Trends

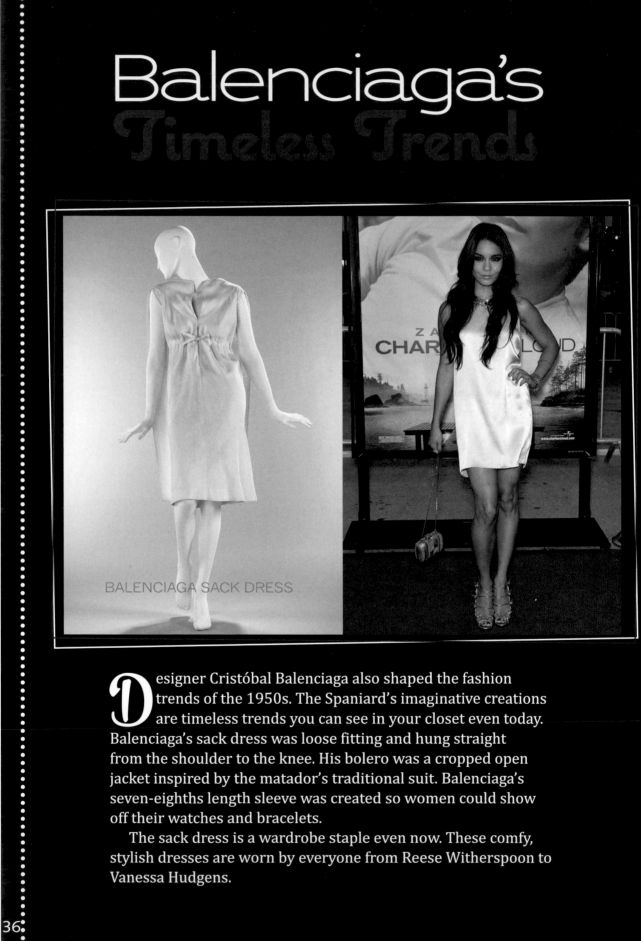

BALENCIAGA SACK DRESS

Designer Cristóbal Balenciaga also shaped the fashion trends of the 1950s. The Spaniard's imaginative creations are timeless trends you can see in your closet even today. Balenciaga's sack dress was loose fitting and hung straight from the shoulder to the knee. His bolero was a cropped open jacket inspired by the matador's traditional suit. Balenciaga's seven-eighths length sleeve was created so women could show off their watches and bracelets.

The sack dress is a wardrobe staple even now. These comfy, stylish dresses are worn by everyone from Reese Witherspoon to Vanessa Hudgens.

Get the Look

In the 1950s eyeglasses and sunglasses became accessories. Designers created pointed and winged frames that were especially popular. You can make your own cat-eye glasses to get the retro look.

SUPPLIES

- pencil
- ruler
- unlined paper
- scissors
- 1 pair black wayfarer sunglasses

- 4-inch (10-cm) square piece of faux leather in your choice of color
- a permanent marker in a color matching the faux leather
- hot glue gun and glue

1. Draw a 1-inch high by ¾-inch wide (2.5x2-cm) crescent shape on the paper. Cut out the shape. Then write an "L" on it.
2. Hold the shape to the left eyepiece on the sunglasses. The top and bottom points of the crescent should match up with the outside shape of the glasses. Trim the shape to fit, if needed.
3. Flip the crescent shape over, and trace it on your paper. Cut the shape out. Draw an "R" on this shape.
4. Place your paper patterns on the leather. Trace around the patterns with the marker.
5. Cut out the leather pieces.
6. Glue the leather pieces on the sunglasses. If you wish, embellish the leather with beads. Let the glue dry before wearing your sweet shades.

THE RISE OF TEEN FASHION

At school young men and women were expected to follow a strict dress code. Full circle skirts influenced by Dior with starched crinoline petticoats and sweater sets were typically worn by girls. Girls were often forbidden to wear pants.

But outside of school, teens began to rebel. For the first time in history, teens started dressing less like their parents and more like pop culture celebrities. Two things brought celeb styles to 1950s teens—TV and rock 'n' roll.

The invention of TV made a huge impact on style. TV showed viewers what was happening around the world. They saw the newest Parisian fashions on the *Today Show*. They watched their favorite singers belt out songs. And for the first time, people saw commercials for apparel and cosmetics—and they bought what was advertised to them. Sound familiar?

In 1951 DJ Alan Freed debuted his show, *Moondog Rock 'n' Roll Party*, spinning pop rhythm and blues music. Freed introduced rock and roll sounds to radio listeners. The sounds of rock and roll were life-changing for teens. So beloved was the new American music scene that youth fashion worldwide was influenced by it. In America rock and roll was the sound of rebellion and independence.

Many of the new rock and roll stars, including Elvis Presley, sported a unique look. They wore a variation of the zoot suit paired with the look of a "greaser." Zoot suits were made famous by jazz musicians in the '30s and '40s. These suits combined high-waisted trousers with baggy jackets. The term "greaser" comes from the greasy look that hair gel gave a guy's hair.

TYPICAL 1950S SCHOOL OUTFIT

Get the Look

The classic black and white saddle shoes that school girls wore are a must-have 1950s look.

SUPPLIES

- a pair of clean white canvas tennis shoes with laces
- a black fabric marker
- a can of acrylic gloss spray

1. Remove the laces from the shoes, and set them aside.
2. Use the marker to draw an outline on one side of a shoe, following the stitch lines that go along the toe and heel areas. Then color in the section. Repeat on the other side. Don't color the tongue, toe, heel, or sole of the shoe.
3. Repeat step 2 on the second shoe.
4. Spray the shoes lightly with an acrylic gloss spray.
5. Let the shoes dry for 24 hours before lacing and wearing them.

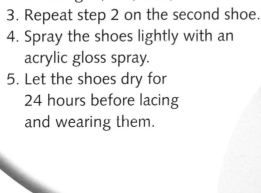

This look showed the world they didn't follow the rules.

JAMES DEAN

ZAC EFRON

Several stars took the greaser look to another level. They paired their gelled hair with crumpled T-shirts, leather jackets, and jeans. This look showed the world they didn't follow the rules of dressing and acting like society wanted them to. Stars including Marlon Brando in the movie *The Wild One* and James Dean in *Rebel Without a Cause* didn't want boundaries. They, and many teenagers, wanted the freedom to dress and act however they wanted. Some people called these rebels "hoods," short for hoodlum or outlaw.

The "hood" look is a classic 1950s style. Teens danced to rock and roll wearing sneakers and rolled-up blue jeans. Today the look is as popular as it was then. Katie Holmes, Kate Hudson, Selena Gomez, and Vanessa Hudgens have all pulled off the dungaree look with '50s inspired boyfriend jeans. Zac Efron, Chace Crawford, and Taylor Lautner have been photographed with the ever popular rebel chic T-shirt and leather jacket.

PUT IT TOGETHER

The hood look is a timeless and very comfy look. You might just be able to pull an outfit together from pieces you already own.

Turn your favorite pair of jeans into '50s style. Just fold the pant legs into cuffs that fall just above your ankles.

Hit up the thrift store to find a long-sleeve plaid shirt. Roll up the sleeves for a retro look.

Ask your grandma if she has any short scarves. Tie one off to the side of your neck to really polish off the look.

Penny loafers were a huge 1950s trend. If you can't find those, loafers in fun colors or even simple flats will work just fine.

Jazz singer Billie Holiday made the hair flower famous in the '30s and '40s. It was still a popular accessory in the 1950s. You can find them at any accessory store.

Get the Look

During the 1950s Americans went crazy for poodles. Poodles were so popular that images of them appeared on everything from playing cards to skirts. Make a poodle skirt, and pair it with a polo shirt and saddle shoes, to really bring back the '50s.

SUPPLIES

- 48-inch (122-cm) square of felt, your choice of color
- measuring tape
- a piece of chalk or a marker
- fabric scissors
- 1 package iron-on Velcro
- 7-inch (18-cm) square of black or white felt
- hot glue gun and glue
- 25 inches (64 cm) of ¼-inch (.6-cm) wide ribbon, your choice of color
- 1 plastic googly eye

1. Lay the large felt square flat on a cutting surface. Fold the left edge over to the right edge. Then fold the top edge down to the bottom edge to create a 24-inch (61-cm) square.
2. Draw a curved line from the top left corner to the bottom right corner. Cut along that line. Unfold the felt.
3. Fold the felt into a half circle with folded edge on top. Then, fold the left side over the right side.
4. Measure 4 inches (10 cm) from the left side corner across the top fold and make a mark. Then measure 4 inches (10 cm) from the top corner down the left-side fold and make another mark. Draw a rounded line to connect the marks. Cut along the line to make a waist hole.
5. Open the skirt into a circle again. Cut a straight line from the bottom of the skirt to the waist hole.
6. Cut two 2-inch (5-cm) long pieces of Velcro.

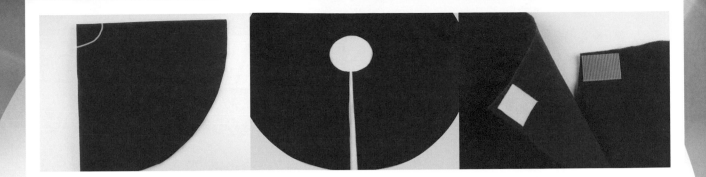

7. Try on the skirt and mark where the ends meet to comfortably fit your waist. Follow the directions on the Velcro package to apply one piece of Velcro on the outside of the skirt and the other on the inside matching your mark.

8. Find a poodle printable online and print it. Cut out the printable. Lay the poodle pattern on the square of felt and trace it. Cut the poodle out of the felt.

9. Make a mark on the skirt where you want the middle of the poodle to go. Hot glue one end of the ribbon to the mark. Continue gluing the ribbon up the skirt, adding loops in the ribbon as you go. Tuck the ribbon over the waistband and glue in place.

10. Glue the poodle over the ribbon on the dot you made. Then glue on the dog's googly eye.

GETTING ACTIVE

As middle class families had more money and time for traveling, people wanted more casual clothes to wear for their "down time." Continuing her success into the '50s, Claire McCardell started designing relaxed leisure and sportswear. These casual fashions moved away from the "high society" and well-to-do prices of the Paris and New York runways. People didn't need to pay expensive designer prices for their leisure wear. Once again, McCardell's fashions were available in department stores in a variety of reasonable prices for all budgets.

Designers experimented with fabrics to make comfortable, fun clothing for the new active lifestyles. They used stretch fabrics, bright colors, florals, plaids, and animal prints. Women enjoyed playsuits, beach dresses, and cover-ups. McCardell marketed summer wear separates that included coordinating sleeveless sun tops, skirts, and shorts. Aloha shirts became quite a fad for men. Collared polo-style shirts and Bermuda shorts also became fashionable.

People wanted more casual clothes to wear for their "down time."

The trends found in today's beachwear are obvious throwbacks to the 1950s. Clothing stores everywhere sell Bermuda shorts and polo shirts. McCardell's sleeveless sun tops are today's tanks.

And what's summer without bright colors and Aloha shirts and dresses?

KATY PERRY

KATHARINE MCPHEE

Sporty Styles

During wartime women didn't just keep the factories going. They were recruited to keep sports fans entertained too. These athletes led the way to many groundbreaking styles that are still with us today.

1943

More than 500 women were recruited to play pro baseball for the All-American Girls Baseball League. Players wore baseball caps, jerseys, and cute short skirts. They were also required to wear lipstick and nail polish to keep their ladylike look.

1946

Louis Réard invented the bikini. The garment's name came from the Bikini Atoll, a nuclear testing site in the South Pacific. It was named for the "explosive" effect it had on anyone looking at it. Too skimpy for women at that time, it remained unpopular until the '50s.

Of course, this style is hot today. Tabloid mags are always snapping shots of A-listers in their tiny bikinis.

1948

Swim champion and movie star Esther Williams partnered with Cole of California company. They introduced bathing suits made of Lastex, a revolutionary fabric made of rubber and nylon. Lastex made suits lightweight and fast drying. Before this time suits were made of cotton or wool.

Actress Bridget Bardot helped promote a more modest bikini. The charming floral print covered to the waist and was more like shorts with a cropped tank top.

The high-waisted bikini is making a comeback. Taylor Swift, Bella Thorne, and Ke$ha have all taken a dip in this retro fashion.

1953

early 1950s

Teenage girls began to dominate the sport of cheerleading. Before World War II, cheerleading was very popular with young men. Female cheerleaders adopted mid-calf length skirts worn with letterman sweaters and saddle shoes. As the years went on, cheerleading skirts have gotten shorter and more versatile. But they are still throwbacks to the first ones worn in the 1950s.

CAPRIS and Pedal Pushers

By the end of the 1950s, new active lifestyles heavily influenced fashion. More and more women wore pants for leisure and casual use. This trend brought about the design of a capri pant. Capris were named after the Italian island Capri because of its relaxed and active atmosphere. Pedal pushers, which allowed women to comfortably push bike pedals, also exploded in popularity.

These two styles were very similar. The main difference was length. Pedal pushers went just below the knee. Capris, or clam-diggers as some called them, went to mid-calf. Capris were worn more for beach days or gardening.

Whatever the length, society embraced the use of women's pants in the '50s and never turned back. Today capris are one of the most loved and hated trends around. Nearly every star, from Britney Spears to Heidi Klum, has been spotted wearing them. The term "pedal pushers" has fallen out of favor. Fashion gurus usually call any short pant a capri or cropped pant.

EMMA STONE

Get the Look

The letterman sweater was a major teen fad in the 1950s. Girls wore them as a status symbol, showing they were dating an athlete. Make your own letterman sweater and wear it to show your school spirit. Pair it with a pair of pedal pushers and some flats for a sweet, retro look.

SUPPLIES

- scissors
- two 9x12-inch (23x30-cm) pieces of felt in two coordinating colors
- ruler
- permanent marker
- fabric glue
- a plain sweater or buttoned knit cardigan

1. Using a word processing program, print out a letter that is at least 5 inches (13 cm) tall.
2. Cut out the letter. Make sure to cut out the white parts inside letters such as R or P.
3. Turn the letter over so it's backward, and lay it on a piece of felt. Trace around the letter.
4. Cut out the felt letter, being careful to cut out the parts inside the letter shape too.
5. Turn the felt letter over so it's backward, and lay it on the second piece of felt. Measure ½ inch (1 cm) from the letter's edge and make a mark. Continue measuring and marking all around the letter's outside edge. Connect the marks to make an outline. Don't do this for any interior spots on the letter.
6. Cut out the letter outline shape.
7. Turn the outline shape over, so it looks like the letter you want. Glue the letter to the outline shape. Press the two pieces together until the glue dries.
8. Lay the sweater or cardigan flat on your workspace. If you have a sweater, glue the letter patch to the center of the shirt. If you're using a cardigan, glue the letter to the right side. Press down on the patch until the glue dries.

HAIR *and* MAKEUP

Before the 1940s American women didn't use many cosmetics. Most women simply washed with soap and water then applied cold cream and white powder to their faces. But beginning in the 1940s, primping and the artistic application of cosmetics helped women express themselves. Sweet smelling perfumes, pancake makeup, and lipstick became popular, everyday tools to make women look and feel their best. It was during this time that the fantasy of the "bombshell" was born.

The term "bombshell" originated in the '30s from the platinum haired, red-lipped beauty Jean Harlow. Harlow starred in a movie called *Bombshell*. She was dazzling and flirty—so the name stuck around. By World War II the meaning expanded to redheads and brunettes. These bombshells typically flaunted an hourglass figure, fresh faces, and a lipsticked smile.

JEAN HARLOW

The Ultimate Bombshell

You can't talk about "bombshell" actresses without mentioning the most iconic one of them all—Marilyn Monroe. Monroe wasn't just a 1950s film star. She has become one of the most legendary style icons in the world.

Countless actresses have imitated Monroe's classic look. Scarlett Johansson, Gwen Stefani, and Katherine Heigl have all shown their curves in body-hugging gowns and accented their smiles with bold red lips. Lady Gaga, Madonna, and Christina Aguilera have imitated Monroe's platinum blonde locks.

Monroe wore many memorable dresses. The white pleated halter dress that blew around her in *The Seven Year Itch* sold for $5.6 million at an auction in 2011. Then there's the skin-tight nude-color sequined dress she wore when singing "Happy Birthday" to President John F. Kennedy. She was quite literally sewn into that dress. And countless stars have followed in her fashion footsteps.

But possibly Monroe's biggest fashion contribution wasn't what she wore, but how she wore it. Monroe was daring and scandalous in her day. She knew she was beautiful, and she flaunted it.

monroe's glamorous style is enduring and timeless. Need proof? Macy's carries a junior clothing line dedicated entirely to her. The store even has a version of the white halter dress. Britney Spears called on Monroe's classic style for her Onyx Hotel Tour, wearing white blonde hair, deep red lips, and diamonds. Even Paris Hilton has worn the classic Marilyn look on the red carpet.

THE LIST GOES
ON AND ON ...

Makeup Explosion

Women needed products to get that bombshell look. Lipstick was the first product to really fly off the shelves. By the beginning of the 1940s, ladies applied lipstick more than they brushed their teeth!

During the '40s teens wore the lipstick pout, copying stars such as Rita Hayworth and Veronica Lake. The lipstick pout accentuated the lips. Fashionista Joan Crawford was known to apply lipstick past her natural lip lines, doubling their size.

Actresses of the time also wore greasepaint created by Max Factor. Factor made flexible greasepaint in a wide range of shades that helped make actresses look more natural in close-ups for film. These greasepaints were called pancake makeup. The thick, oily cream, applied with a sponge, covered acne, freckles, and scars, creating a flawless complexion. The actresses looked so stunning that women everywhere were asking for the makeup too. The products became available to the public in the late 1930s. And by the 1950s they were in widespread, everyday use. Today liquid and powder foundation have replaced greasepaint. The products may have changed, but the goal of flawless complexions is still the same.

Women in the 1950s wore their brows thick and generously penciled in. The feline, or cat eye, became a staple in eye makeup, swooping toward the temple and enlarging the look of the eye using a brow pencil. Eye shadows also started to be produced at this time.

By the late 1950s every woman was influenced by Audrey Hepburn's dark doe eyes that were shadowed, lined, and plumped with mascara.

The cat eye and doe eye looks are still popular today. Nicole Scherzinger and Kim Kardashian have both flashed cat eyes. Emmy Rossum and Katy Perry are just two of the countless celebs who keep the doe eye look going.

AUDREY HEPBURN
1956

Get the *Look*

Give your makeup routine a boost of retro with the doe eye look.

SUPPLIES

- shimmery, light-colored eye shadow
- darker eye shadow, complimenting the lighter one
- black eyeliner pencil or liquid liner
- eyelash curler
- black mascara

1. Apply light colored eye shadow on both eyelids. Also lightly apply it on both sides of the bridge of your nose.
2. Apply a darker shadow in the creases of your eyelids.
3. Underline the lower lashes with an unbroken line of eyeliner.
4. Curl your lashes. Then apply two coats of mascara. Make sure it doesn't get clumpy.

EMMY ROSSUM
2013

Nail Art

Fingernail polish grew in popularity in the 1940s. Elite socialites in Paris set this trend. They were photographed summering on the Rivera with blood-red nail varnish.

American women introduced their own trend of wearing black nail polish. Interestingly, this trend can be linked to American automobile icon Henry Ford. Ford used fast-drying lacquer to paint his cars. To keep costs low, he only used black. As the popularity of Ford's automobiles grew, so did the popularity of the color they were painted. Black is back for modern trendsetters too. Everyone from Solange to Fergie has worn this nail color.

The half-moon manicure was a popular trend in the '50s. Women painted their nails, leaving the bottom quarter of the nail unpainted. Of course, nail art has grown to new heights today. Celebs and everyday women paint their nails every color of the rainbow. And the idea of painting cool shapes or pictures on the nails is an amazing throwback trend.

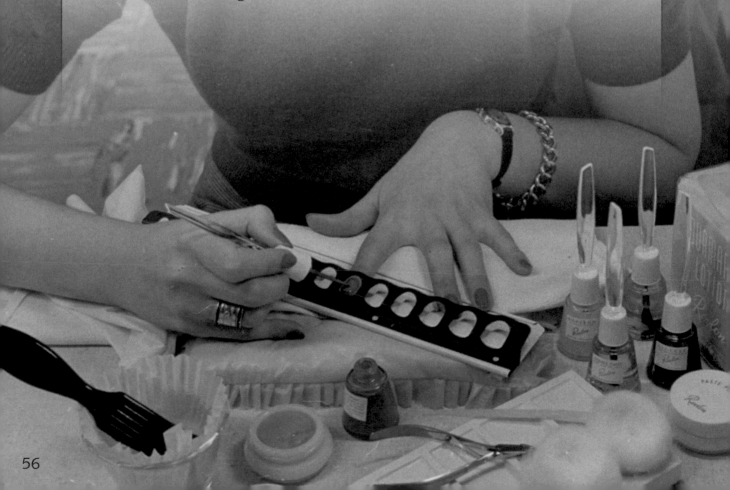

Get the *Look*

Re-create the classic half-moon mani for yourself.

SUPPLIES

- polish remover
- adhesive hole reinforcing rings
- fire-engine red or jet-black nail polish
- clear coat nail polish

1. Clean your nails with polish remover.
2. Place a reinforcing ring on the bottom fourth of each nail.
3. Paint your nails bright red or black. You can paint right over the rings.
4. When the polish is still slightly wet, carefully remove the rings.
5. Let your half-moons dry, and then apply a clear coat. Dry completely.

Timeless Tresses

The most popular hairstyle of the '40s was the "peek-a-boo" cut made popular by actress Veronica Lake. The sultry hairdo fell just past the shoulders and covered one eye. Women everywhere started wearing this simple look. But it was impractical for factory workers who kept getting their hair caught in machinery.

The U.S. government's war department actually asked Lake to style her hair differently for the safety of workers!

Many stars still wear the timeless, gorgeous peek-a-boo style. Julianne Moore and Jennifer Lawrence are just two people who've blown viewers away with this simply lovely look.

VERONICA LAKE

Get the *Look*

A major hair trend in the '50s was the greaser pompadour hair style. The pompadour is particularly hot right now for both men and women. Jenny McCarthy, P!nk, and Rihanna have all shown off this high-flying style.

SUPPLIES

- thin spaced comb with a thin rat-tail end
- claw clip
- bobby pins
- hair spray

1. Make a part on the top of your head in a horseshoe shape. Clip the hair on top of the head with a claw clip.
2. Twist the rest of your hair in the back into a simple bun. Use bobby pins to pin it in place.
3. Unclip the hair at the top of your head and lay it back over the bun.
4. Use the rat-tail end of the comb to grab a 1-inch (2.5-cm) section of hair from the front. Hold the hair straight out from the head. Starting at the middle point of the hair section, comb down the hair toward your head. This will tease the roots into more height. When you're done, leave the hair hanging down over your face.
5. Grab another 1-inch (2.5-cm) section of hair from behind the first section. Tease that hair.

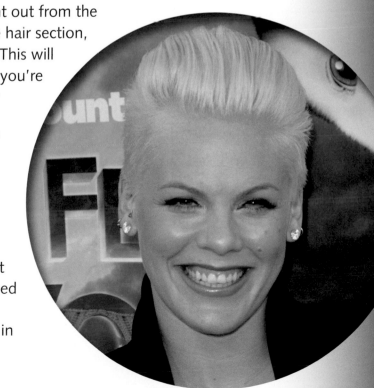

6. Repeat teasing the hair in sections until you have done all the hair that isn't in the bun.
7. Carefully lift the teased hair up and lay it back on the head. Gently comb the teased hair back to smooth it out.
8. Pin the ends of the hair around the bun in the back.
9. Spray with hair spray to set the style.

WEARING THE PROOF

Some fashion historians consider the 1940s and 1950s a turning point in style and culture. In those two decades, Americans defined who they were as a nation and evolved a style that is still prevalent today. The fashion of those decades changed not only how people dressed, but how society viewed beauty.

The trends that would shock in the 1960s and 1970s were deeply influenced by styles invented in the '40s and '50s. And teens' rebellion agaist wearing clothes like their parents would lead to a culture of rebelliousness in the decades to come.

Glossary

A-line (A-LINE)—having a triangular shape; A-line skirts are fitted around the waist and flare at the sides

bias cut (BYE-uhs CUT)—a way of cutting fabric that is diagonal to the grain of the fabric

bodice (BOD-uhs)—the upper part of a garment between the waist and the shoulders

couture (koo-TUR)—fashionable clothing that is custom-made

crinoline (KRIN-oh-lin)—a full, stiff underskirt

girdle (gur-DUHL)—a women's undergarment worn around the waist

hem (HEM)—a border of a cloth garment that is doubled back and stitched down

petticoat (peh-tee-KOT)—an underskirt often made with a ruffled, pleated, or lace edge

sheath (SHEETH)—a close-fitting dress usually worn without a belt

stocking (STOK-ing)—a tight, knitted covering for the foot and leg

stole (STOL)—a long, wide scarf or other covering worn across the shoulders

zoot suit (ZOOT SOOT)—a suit consisting of a thigh-length jacket with padded shoulders and narrow pants with cuffs

Read More

Behnke, Alison Marie. *The Little Black Dress and Zoot Suits: Depression and Wartime Fashions from the 1930s to 1950s.* Dressing a Nation—The History of U.S. Fashion. Minneapolis.: Twenty-First Century Books, 2012.

Niven, Felicia Lowenstein. *Fabulous Fashions of the 1940s.* Fabulous Fashions of the Decades. Berkeley Heights, N.J.: Enslow Publishers, Inc., 2012.

Sonneborn, Liz. *Far Out Fashion: Bringing 1960s and 1970s Flair to Your Wardrobe.* Fashion Forward. North Mankato, Minn.: Capstone Press, 2014.

Internet Sites

FactHound offers a safe, fun way to find Internet sites related to this book. All of the sites on FactHound have been researched by our staff.

Here's all you do:

Visit *www.facthound.com*

Type in this code: 9781476539980

 Check out projects, games and lots more at
www.capstonekids.com

Index